Chelsea's Heart

Chelsea's Heart

DR. WANDA C. YOUNG AND CHELSEA DENISE YOUNG

Mark 5:41
And having laid hold of the hand of the child, he says to her, Talitha kokumi, which is, interpreted, Damsel, I say to thee, Arise.

Chelsea's Heart

Copyright © 2019 by Dr. Wanda C. Young and Chelsea Denise Young.
All rights reserved.

No part of this publication may be reproduced, stored in a retrieval system or transmitted in any way by any means, electronic, mechanical, photocopy, recording or otherwise without the prior permission of the author except as provided by USA copyright law.

The opinions expressed by the author are not necessarily those of URLink Print and Media.

1603 Capitol Ave., Suite 310 Cheyenne, Wyoming USA 82001
1-888-980-6523 | admin@urlinkpublishing.com

URLink Print and Media is committed to excellence in the publishing industry.

Book design copyright © 2019 by URLink Print and Media. All rights reserved.

Published in the United States of America

ISBN 978-1-64367-564-0 (Paperback)
ISBN 978-1-64367-563-3 (Digital)

Non-Fiction
12.06.19

CONTENTS

Introduction..7
Chapter 1: A Sure Foundation 11
Chapter 2: I Am Entitled to It 17
Chapter 3: When I Met God For Real 20
Chapter 4: Champions Train for Championships.......................25
Chapter 5: The blessing of being connected to godly people......28
Chapter 6: Chelsea's Delima...................................30
Chapter 7: God Gave Hannah Samuel; He gave us MJ:.............38
Chapter 8: Talitha Cumin 42
Chapter 9: Write the Vision 45

Chelsea TELLS HER STORY...................................49

INTRODUCTION

Finally, the Spirit of God has given me permission to release this inspirational work in print. Throughout my travels and speaking opportunities, God has allowed me to share my testimony and my faith in Him with many people. This book is especially important to me because I am excited to finally be able to share my heart in print. As you read the following pages, you will witness a real account of how God demonstrated his unconditional love to me and my family. Our family is made up of five amazing people: Marvin (dad), Wanda (mom), MJ (big brother), Chelsea (our miracle), and Jada (our baby). We are better known to our friends and family as the Young family. Some parts of this story may seem unreal, but I assure you, every printed word is true. For the last few years, my family members, friends, and co-workers have continued to encourage me to publish this testimony so that others will know that I have experienced the power of God in my life for real. These precious friends, family, and co-workers are dear to my heart and their constant encouragement has provoked me to tell our story. At times, I wanted to go ahead and send the transcript to the publisher, but in my spirit, I could hear the Lord saying to me, "Wait". "Not yet". "I have more that I want to say to you." I have learned to hear and obey the voice of God because I have come to realize the true meaning of the scripture found in I Samuel 15:22 "…obedience is better than sacrifice." (King James Version)

First of all, I want to say a special thank you to my dear friends and prayer partners who have helped me to write this book: Dee, Phyllis, Mildred, Joy, Pam and Sister Linda. Thank you all for your constant prayers and words of encouragement. Your friendship means so much to me. Thank you for helping me to stay focused and for helping me to realize that God's timing is always perfect. I release this testimony of God's love to the Young family in the name of Jesus. Let the words of this message leap from this page into the hearts of the reader and take root. My prayer is that for years to come, people all over the globe who read this testimony and people all over the land will be saved and filled with the Holy Spirit in Jesus Name.

Here is a little bit of my story: In my 30's I had three children. Like most women in their 30's, I had many roles to fill: mother, wife, sister, care taker for elderly family members, a student, choir member, church worker, high school teacher, club adviser, and added to all of these roles was the role of mother to my amazing 3 kids. For nearly 3 and a half years, I faced the fact that my major job was the nurturing of my children and helping them become independent adults. Well, that's not too abnormal considering that millions of other women were doing the same thing. What makes this story different and interesting is that these 3 kids were all born with health concerns. The truth was that I have 3 sick babies. All 3 were born with life threating medical situations from birth.

God allowed me to walk through the times when Marvin and I faced multiple surgeries, childhood cancer, years of chemotherapy, long trips to doctor's appointments and many other things related to getting my children healthy. However, God allowed us to experience so many amazing things during this time. My faith was tested on so many levels. God not only carried me through this season of my life, but he also allowed me to see His healing power restore the love that was needed to heal a sick, marriage that was headed for divorce. Not only was our marriage strengthened, but our faith in God and his promises allowed us to remain stable and employed even despite the challenges. God did not allow the circumstances of our situations to overtake us. One thing that really amazed me as I reflect on this time in my life was the fact that even though our circumstances often called for my husband and I to miss work, both of us were able to keep our jobs and maintain our benefits. Along with the health issues, my husband and I, together as a couple, experienced a terribly embarrassing legal ordeal that was surely meant to shatter or family's foundation forever.

My husband and I were headed for a divorce, our property was one month before foreclosure, and we were headed for bankruptcy. We endured exposure of our personal challenges and on one occasion, our personal business issues were printed in the local newspaper. We live in a small town, so everyone knew what was going on in our life. I felt so ashamed and all alone. I felt like I was clinging to life without a rope! There were times that I was ashamed to go in the grocery store for fear that someone would stop me and want to talk. I was depressed and on my way to a mental institution.

How much more could I take of all this pain? After all, I am saved and I know in my heart that I love the Lord and that he loves me. So why is this happening to me? And did I mention already that none of the children were expected to live. You may wonder and this point, what is going on in my life? What am I supposed to learn from all of these issues? The answers to these and other questions surrounding my testimony are answered throughout this work. Please hear my heart and know that my story is real and it reassures me that God is not just someone to read about, that He is very much alive and he does hear and answer the prayers of the believer.

This book is an absolute true account of events that I experienced in my life. The things that happened to me and my family members were challenging and at times they seemed impossible to overcome, but my faith in God allowed me to stand on the word of God in spite of these difficulties. I was victorious in every situation and to God be the glory for all the wonderful things that He has done for the Young family.

As I look back and recall these events, I believe with all my heart, that God Himself trained me and my family to become true champions for Christ. He used the trials and triumphs to show me his perfect plan for my life and the life of my family. What I learned during this difficult time in my life is that God is faithful and his love for me—and for you— is amazing.

It is my prayer that as you read the pages of this book, you will experience the love and faithfulness of our Lord and Savior Jesus Christ showed to my family. I pray that your faith will come alive as you read about the Godly relationship that I experienced even in my trials. You will come to know how I drew closer to God and I came to know and trust him in a very special way.

CHAPTER 1

A Sure Foundation

I am a firm believer that the source of stability in a healthy family is evident when the family's values, decisions, and beliefs are based on the love of God and the Word of God. It is a real blessing to raise children in such a way that they will love and serve God and allow their hearts to be trained to become champions for the Lord. A true champion can be described as a one who has earned the right to be called a winner, an overcomer, and a titleholder. A true champion lives from his heart; Champions overcome adversity with their can-do attitude. A champion is one who must be able to stand on a firm foundation.

If a child is to grow and be trained to become a champion for Christ, he must be led by a champion. My life has been compared to that of a champion in training because I was blessed in my childhood with so many people who helped me grow up strong and solid. They taught me how to stand in the face of adversity, no matter what situation I encountered. I am so blessed to have been trained to never, ever quit. Giving up was and never will be an option for me. The people who raised me during my childhood were great matriarchs with keen direction and forward thinking. They were always able to do what my Pastor calls "look at the big picture" in any situation. They were confident in themselves and in their God.

They understood that their job was to produce and to raise a strong generation to carry the torch. I believe they fulfilled their calling.

I did not grow up in what you might call a typical home; but it was the plan that God had for my life. My champion foundation came from the strength that I was taught as a child while I was growing up in the rural South in the early 1960's and 1970's. During this time, little black girls, like myself, were not thought of as champions. We were, at best, expected to follow in the footsteps of our mothers and grandmothers and become domestic servants to the white families that our mothers and grandmothers had worked for all their lives. The torch was passed alright, but that torch was lateral. What I mean by that is, little black girls in the south during this time when I was a girl could only dream of becoming a few things other than a maid or housekeeper, or a good cook. As I reflect on the women in my family on both sides, I see that my mother's mother was a farmhand. My great grandmother was also a tobacco farmer's wife. Both women were uneducated and there were no expectations to advance to anything different. On my father's side of my family, his mother was a cotton field-hand and she would also sometimes keep the children who were too young to work in the fields. My great-grandmother was a mid-wife and also a farmer's wife. Her mother, my great-great grandmother was born in slavery and worked on a cotton plantation in Kingstree, South Carolina as a field hand herself. She was paid $.25 a day no matter how much cotton she picked. The one thing that was consistent throughout my lineage was the strength of the women that proceeded me and their love and desire for their children and grandchildren to get an education. It is one of the amazing legacies that was passed on to my generation.

My parents arrived on the scene in the early 1920's and collectively their parents had passed the torch to my parents to excel in life through knowing God, studying the bible, and getting an education. It is interesting what God did with my parents for the first 15 years of their married life. My parents, Ulysses Samuel Carter and Truth Mae Singletary Carter were married in the summer of 1954. They met at Greater St. Paul Baptist Church in Waycross Georgia. The pastor at that time was, Rev. Eugene James Menefee. My father was a young railroad worker who had followed in his own dad's footsteps to land a job working for the famous Southern railroad transportation system known at that time as the Atlantic Coastline Railroad. The ACL, as it was called, was the largest employer in the southeast and the major employer in my small town of Waycross Georgia. My father held several jobs at the railroad, a laborer, a cook, a wrecker worker, an extra-board worker and other jobs as needed. Of course, he was a dedicated, hardworking man who provided well for his family.

I remember very well that it seemed that my daddy was always working. He spent many hours working overtime and traveling to various parts of the south to cook for the railroad workers who were called out to clean up after a train derailed or some other type of train trouble had occurred. What I recall most about my father is that he was a man of vision. He had a clear plan of where he wanted his family, his business, and his life to be over the next decade. He owned real estate in our town and he was the proud owner of his own small-town grocery store and fish market. He became affectional known as the "snow ball" man and the "fish" market man. He was a morally good man who served the community and also served as the head of the deacon board at the church. He was young, successful, and most of all, he was single. Friends and family described him as a quiet, kind, and a very attentive man especially to his blind mother. My father was the only living child to his blind mother- Roxie Cooper Carter (December 1, 1897-October 25, 1997). His siblings proceeded him in death. His sister died as an infant before her 1st birthday and his baby brother died when he was thrown from a horse around his 17th birthday. My father was very good to his mother and they lived together happily and peacefully until his death in 1970.

One of the other families in the church, Moses and Edna Moore, were housing Edna's 25-year-old beautiful niece from Bladenboro North Carolina, Trudah Singletary. Trudah was the oldest girl of 8 children born to Hobart and Pasavior (Faulk) Singletary. Trudah's parents had high expectation of her. She was to move to Georgia and teach school during the school year and during the summer months she was to return to Bladenboro to help her parents and younger siblings work the fields on the family-owned tobacco farm. Trudah had moved to Georgia with the intention of teaching elementary school in Georgia for two years. Prior to the desegregation of schools in the south, Georgia had fewer teacher employment requirements than North Carolina. Trudah met the requirements because she had completed two years at the North Carolina Teacher's College. Trudah could teach in Georgia, and live with her aunt and uncle and so she moved to Georgia. The plan was that after two years of teaching experience in Georgia, she could return to North Carolina and she would then qualify as a certified teacher in her home state of North Carolina. The plan was in place and off to the rural south she went. Trudah was young, single, healthy, smart ambitions and she was very pretty.

As fate would have it, the pastor of the church, Rev. Menefee, introduced Ulysses to Trudah. The relationship started slowly over the next two years. The couple dated, fell in love, and were married in the summer of 1954. This was the beginning of the family; Ulysses, Trudah, and Ulysses' blind mother, Mama Roxie. Trudah continued to travel back to Bladenboro during the summers to help her mom and dad and younger siblings on the farm, but each time she returned, one more person was added to the trip. Reginald was born first in 1956, Syble was born next in 1958, and finally, I was born last in 1960.

Our family did not thrive but a few years after I was born. My mother died of Sarcoidosis when I was five years old. My father died of kidney failure when I was ten years old. After both of my parents were gone, my blind grandmother faced the decision as to whether or not to send the three of us off to live with other relatives or try to raise her 3 grandchildren by herself. She chooses to keep us because she said God told her that she had His help. She often spoke of the dream she had as a young woman in her early 40's. She shared that an angel appeared to her one night and said to her, "Go back to younger's world, it is not your time yet for you to come up to Heaven now, you have not completed your assignment. God gave you three things to do here on earth." I finally asked her one day what were the three things to do. She quietly said to me, you are one, Ricky and

Syble together make up the other 2 and together you are the 3 things I had to do. Mama Roxie said that God spoke to her and told her, your assignment is to raise these 3 children by teaching them about me (God), giving them a good education, and teaching them the value of a strong family. Mama Roxie died in 1997 at the age of 100. She fulfils her assignment that the Lord gave her to do. Ricky, Syble, and I have always remarked about the beautiful life that she lived for the Lord. I was nearly 40 years old when she died. I often think about how amazing to have completed several educational degrees and many other things that I wanted to accomplish and for the first 40 years of my life, I was led by a blind woman.

My father died when I was ten years old. My brother was 14 and my sister was 12. By this time, Mama Roxie was 72 years old. Most people would say that 72 is too old to be responsible for children at this age. My father was the only child to survive. He had grown up without siblings and with the major responsibility of taking care of his blind mother. After my father's died, my grandmother knew that she would need help raising the 3 of us. She had the foresight to get her sister, Etta Mae, to move in with the four of us. Etta Mae was Mama Roxie's youngest sister. They were 10 years apart. They got along really well with each other although they had opposite personalities. Etta Mae had been married before, but she had never had children of her own. She was an excellent cook and knew how to run a house. She could manage money well and she and Mama Roxie teamed up together to get the job done. Etta Mae was faced with the responsibility of having to parent these three children, yet she did not have any experience in this area. She had to learn how to parent teenagers with no prior knowledge. I often think about the fact that my grandmother and my aunt were seventy-two and sixty-two years old when they became parents. Can you imagine being that age and taking on the responsibility of parenting a 14-year-old male, and two girls ages 12 and 10? I am not sure they were thinking, perhaps they just did what had to be done. I do know that both of them were strong, smart, women of faith. They raised us to do well in life.

I am so thankful and grateful to these two women in my life. They were amazing women who provided me and my siblings with a solid foundation in God. Mama Roxie taught me many life lessons, but the lesson that I feel was the most important one is she taught me and my siblings was how to truly fall in love with God. The foundation that I came from was solid in the prayers of mama Roxie and my great-aunt Etta Mae. No matter what they faced in life, they faced it with courage and with prayer. These amazing Women of God who truly had the heart of a champion for Christ. I had a wonderful childhood and I am forever grateful for my meager beginnings.

CHAPTER 2

I Am Entitled to It

Reflecting back on my childhood, we were a well-known, blended family. We were somewhat admired in our small community because to the community members, we as a blended family had weathered many storms and survived to talk about the events. I think about it now and I realize that some of my pain was directly tied to a very deep personal place that I needed healing. The type of healing that only God can give. I needed to let go of the image that I had of myself of always having it together because I thought that it was expected of me. The real truth of the matter was I was hurting and I could barely hold my head up! I knew that God was with me and that he would set me free so that I could move on in my life, but it seemed so far off. I felt like I was in the middle of what felt like a storm. The storm was raging with sick kids, sick marriage, sick finances, sickness was all around me. I was so in need of a "pain reliever". My life felt like a constant thunderstorm. Dark clouds followed me throughout my day to day happenings. I continued to go to work, cook and clean, and attend my weekly services at church, but I was in a constant battle on the inside. I was simply going through the motions.

Prior to this time in my life, I had encountered some struggles. I lost a close friend in a car accident; I had experienced a year of mental anguish due to the emotional demands of my life. I needed

God in a way that I felt like no one could possibly understand, and in all honesty, I did not have anyone that really understood what I was going through at that time. Have you ever felt a certain way, but you couldn't explain why you felt the way that you did? If I did try to explain how I felt to someone, I felt judged and laughed at and very much misunderstood. I did not know people who could or would validate me. Well, that is the place that I was in and there seemed to be nothing that I could do about it. I tried to lean on what was familiar to me. In my past struggles, I would call on my big sister, Syble (Syble Ann Carter Ward, August 11, 1958-December 17, 2016). Syble was quick to judge me and my actions on every level. She was always very quick to point out all of the things that I did or did not do correctly. She held her ground and the "big sister" who always knew best for the "little sister". Syble and I had a really strong bond, but she did not understand the emotional side of her baby sister. There were things that I was going through on an emotional level that she could never understand. I knew that about my sister, and I did not hold it against her. She was a smart and intelligent woman in her own right. Her medical advice to me was valuable beyond words. I would often tease her about the fact that I felt that I could pass Nursing 101 after having been through all that I had been through with the sick babies. Syble was a Registered Nurse with more than 20 years of experience in a variety of medical areas. Even though she was knowledgeable in the medical aspect of what was going on with my children, she could not give me the kind of help that I needed. I needed support and understanding on a day to day basis, but she could not help me.

My big brother whom I refer to as, "Ricky", had always been there to rescue me no matter what. There were times growing up that he took on the role as a father in our home more so than a big brother. He was the eyes and ears for my grandmother and my elderly aunt. He helped us maintain the house and the yards by doing the repairs, painting the house, mowing the grass. We even grew our own vegetables in the back yard. Rick was the tiller of the ground. He was valuable to our household. In 1974, he earned a scholarship to attend Florida A & M University (FAMU). He was 17 years old when he left home. Before he went off to college, he continued to do the necessary things to take care of the Homefront. He maintained and drove the cars, changed the oil, and basically took care of the man duties of the home. He always has been to this day a very caring man who looked out for all 4 of the women in the household. He had great advice and solid prayers, but he did not know what I needed to help me through my journey. Big brother himself had not experienced the things that I was going through. We were and still are very close to this day, but he could not relate to my pain.

What do I need to do, Lord? There were so many questions without answers. All I know how to do is pray. My daily prayer became help me Lord. I began to quote the scriptures that I knew in my heart. Daily I would say to myself: Yet, Nevertheless, and But God. I would repeat it again when I felt myself sinking: Yet, Nevertheless, and But God. These are the words that I have taken from 3 scriptures: "Though you slay me, **yet** will I trust you" (KJV, Job 13:15). "**Nevertheless**, not my will, but thy will be done" (KJV, Mark 14:36). "…**But my God** shall supply all of my needs" (KJV, Genesis 8:

CHAPTER 3

When I Met God For Real

I surrendered my life over to God completely on December 31, 1987. From that time forward, I started going after God in every way that I could. I grew up in a wonderful Baptist Church in my hometown. The members of the congregation were committed to the church and they were committed to the things that they taught. For me, that was great, but somehow, I needed more. I wanted a real experience with God. I fell in love with God when I got saved. I am extremely thankful that God allowed me to grow up healthy in a wonderful Christian home. My grandmother was a woman who believed in prayer. She raised me and both of my siblings in church. I had tried hard throughout my teen and young adult years to live up to the "church-girl" role. I was raised in a Baptist Church with good Christian women who loved their husbands and were good wives and good keepers at home. As far as I could tell, these women lived the Titus 2 life.

Newly saved and ready to take on adulthood, I fell in love and married Marvin Wayne Young on July 23, 1988. We were both ready to start a family right away. I was 28 and Marvin was 34 years old. We believed that children were a part of our union and therefore we started planning for our children in our 3rd year of marriage. I gave birth to my first son in June of 1991, Rupert Samuel Young. Rupert was not alive when he was born. During the pregnancy an infection attacked my body during the first trimester, and therefore Rupert did not live. When I delivered my son, it was 21 weeks into the pregnancy. I was 31 years old.

The days leading up to the delivery were so hard. The doctors told me that the baby was not alive, but I could not believe it. I refused to believe it. I walked around every day trying to convince myself that the baby that I carried for almost 20 weeks was moving on the inside of me. I wanted it so badly, I just could not give up. After all, I am a woman of faith. I believe that anything that I ask God for, he will give it to me. That is what the word of God says and that's what I believe. I refuse to believe anything else. The doctors all said, "No Way, Mrs. Young, the baby that you are carrying is not alive. The body will reject the dead fetus within the next 21 days. I need you to be ready to deliver the baby and to let go."

There is no way I can do that, Oh, no!! Not my child. I talked to everybody about the baby. I felt (looking back) that my family and friends must have believed that I was crazy. I think I literally lost my mind. No one knew the pain I felt. I felt like I had failed God somehow. To be honest, I really wanted to die with my son; it would have been easier than what I was dealing with at that moment. I cried, I mopped, I wined, and I did everything I could do. No matter how much I tried to be depressed, the Lord continued to send me comfort thought His Word. I realize now that the Lord had a different plan for my life. The spirit of God would not let me give up. God has allowed us to experience the hard situation and truth is my first child died.

We were both completely devastated when our little son Rupert Samuel Young was born at 21 weeks. I said a slow painful goodbye to Rupert and waited about 3 years before I had the strength and courage to try to get pregnant again. Even today, nearly 30 years later, I still look around sometime and think one of the children is not home yet. But then I realize that all 3 of them are home. Rupert went home to be with the Lord. I do wish that my son Rupert would have lived, but he didn't. When I started to really pray about having another baby, I was listening for the voice of the Lord one day and I heard the Spirit urging me to do something quickly. I thought for a moment and then I realized: Before I can really receive this promise of children from the Lord, I must first let go of the past. With God's grace and mercy, I was able to totally release the hurt and the pain of losing my baby into the arms of Jesus. My comfort came from the Lord himself. I learned so much about how the Lord works. He says in his word His ways are not our ways. I gained strength in areas of my life that I would have never had if I had not placed all my confidence in the Power of God and in the Word of God. It was a difficult time, but I drew closer to God and I learned that I really can trust him with my heart. To God Be the Glory for the Things that He Has Done in My Life!

One night, I was listening to a gospel TV program and I heard a Pastor teaching on the subject of emotional healing. He started to speak about the servant David and how David's son had died and David found comfort in the Lord when he said that one day, he would hold his child in heaven. I immediately felt the heavy burden that was on my heart lift when the pastor spoke these words.

But when David saw that his servants were whispering together, David understood that the child was dead. And David said to his servants, "Is the child dead?" They said, "He is dead." Then David rose from the earth and washed and anointed himself and changed his clothes. And he went into the house of the Lord and worshiped. He then went to his own house. And when he asked, they set food before him, and he ate. Then his servants said to him, "What is this thing that you have done? You fasted and wept for the child while he was alive; but when the child died, you arose and ate food." He said, "While the child was still alive, I fasted and wept, for I said, "Who knows whether the Lord will be gracious to me, that the child may live?" But now he is dead. Why should I fast? Can I bring him back again? I shall go to him, but he will not return to me" (KJV, 2 Samuel 12:19-23).

My Lord again walked with me every step of the way. The Lord gave me the same promise that he gave to David concerning the death of his baby "I'll hold him in heaven". So, Rupert, my sweet little baby boy, I did have to say goodbye, but one thing that I am sure of and that is I will see you when I get to heaven. I Love you so much and you are always in my heart.

After Rupert died, I started to really go after God. I loved God and I loved to read and study the bible. I love the word of God and I loved reading the stories of other women in the bible who wanted to have babies and they were unable to have them. I was especially interested in Sarah and how God had given her the promise of a child. I began a study of the life of Hannah. I prayed in the same manner the Hannah prayed.

> "And Hannah prayed, and said, my heart rejoiced in the LORD, and mine horn is exalted in the LORD: my mouth is enlarged over mine enemies; because I rejoice in thy salvation. There is none holy as the LORD: for there is none beside thee: neither is there any rock like our God..." (KJV, I Samuel 2:1-2)

In other words, Hannah reminded God of how powerful he was and as she "delighted herself in him, he gave her the desires of her heart" (KJV, Psalm 37:4-5). Believing God for a child became my goal. I reasoned within myself that if the woman of God from the bible, Hannah could evoke God with prayers from her heart to bless her with a child, then surely, I could have the same request, and so I prayed a sincere prayer from my heart and I knew God would not let me down. I knew that I would get a child. God had promised it in his word and so he did just what he said he was going to do. As the years rolled on, we gained strength and courage to try again to conceive a child and M.J. was born, and a few years later, we tried again and Chelsea was born. I guess for me becoming a wife and a mother represented success and I pursued it with all my heart. We were both very excited.

We had become a real family. God blessed us with 3 beautiful miracles. Our son Marvin, Jr., whom we all call M.J., was born in 1994, our oldest daughter Chelsea Denise was born in 1997, and our youngest daughter, Jada Elizabeth was born in 2001. These 3 children were our heritage. The challenges that we endured after our children were born is nothing short of a miracle. MJ, Chelsea, and Jada are alive today because of the grace and mercy of God. Jada was born with one leg slightly shorter than the other leg. When she was 4 months old, God used Jada in a revival service to demonstrate his power. Jada's leg grew instantly in a revival service at my church, Family Worship Center. More than 200 people witnessed this miracle. Our son, M.J. is a beautiful example of what God can and will do even in the face of cancer. When MJ was 3 years old, he was diagnosed with a form of leukemia, which is also known as a rare form of childhood cancer. By the grace of God, MJ was able to endure successfully 3 years of intense chemotherapy to correct the blood disorder that attacked his body. He now lives cancer free since the age of 3. Our daughter, Chelsea was born with a congenital heart defect. She was diagnosed at 5 weeks old with CHARGE syndrome. You may be wondering, how in the world does a mama deal with so many things at one time. A full-time classroom teacher, a wife, a mother, a church worker, and at that time taking care of two elderly people. My grandmother who raised me; Mama Roxie, age 97, and my grandmother's sister, Etta Mae age 87.

Looking back on these times in my life, I can honestly say that I believe that the Lord used these experiences in my life to show my family (and your family if you will receive it) how wonderful he is and how faithful he is to <u>His **Word**.</u> I love the song, "How Great Thou Art" Yes, that's right, you heard me right. God can and did use these experiences to show me how <u>*wonderful he is and how faithful he is*</u> to his promises.

CHAPTER 4

Champions Train for Championships

In my heart, I believed that I had been walking in faith since my salvation on December 31, 1987. So, here we are 10 years later and I have what was I thought the most precious thing in my life other than the Lord, Marvin, and M.J. I really felt complete.

One day, I cried this prayer out to God: Lord Help me stand, help me walk this out! Lord I can't make it without you. I want my life back! Over and Over again, I would cry out to God. Then one day, a thought came to my mind. I had an answer. I had asked God to help me stand and walk this situation out, and he answered me. The thought that came to my mind was simple, "You can't start walking until you stand up. So, that was what I called my step one. I need to stand up or stand on something first before I could begin to walk out of something. I needed something firm, and something sure. I had to get squarely fitted on my foundation, stand on it, and then begin walking through my journey. I searched the word of God to find my right to my victory. I wanted to be sure that I was guaranteed that life for me and my family can be free from sickness, disease and lack. So, I decided that first, I must make sure that I am standing and entitled to what I am asking for. I was right. God's word declares that I can live a blessed life.

My prayer times would sound something like this, "Ok Lord, I am standing on your word that declares that I can have what I say and I say I am blessed." Although my heart was speaking and calling the blessing into my life, I still got up every day and faced the daily challenges of have to care for my sick babies and my sick marriage, and my sick finances! What do I do, Lord?

Two Sick Babies—No bitterness – just peace

It was obvious that they were going to have to do surgery to correct the problems on both of the children. Two babies in the hospital at the same time. What will we do???? How will we cope?? Who? What? When? Oh, the mental anguish that I felt. It seemed like medical science did not have any answers for me. I felt myself slipping and falling apart. On the outside, I appeared to be ok. My friends and co-workers would remark, "Girl, how do you do it?" You look like you got it so together. Sometimes I would wonder to myself, how do I do this? Just looking back on the situation, now I realize that it was just the hand of God and the spirit of God that surrounded me and kept me from going "off "and literally losing my mind. I am so grateful for God's mercy. It would have been very easy at this point to get angry with God, the doctors, my husband, my co-workers and even my students, but I knew that was not the way to handle this situation. In my heart, I made a sound decision that I would not allow strife and bitterness to overtake me. I will not tell you that it was not very tempting, but I chose to be at peace. I would quote the word of God that said, "He will keep you in perfect peace whose mind is stayed on Him" (KJV)

If I lose everything including these children and my husband, I still want you, God

The one thing that I knew that I had to do was I had to give God praise. Yes, Praise. I had to tell God every day and all day in my mind and in my spirit what I thought about Him. I remember that I reached a point while I was driving down the road on my way home from the hospital one day and I was just giving God praises and I said to God, "Lord, if you take these two precious children on to heaven with you right now, I guess all I would be able to do is to just keep on praising you. I told God that I would not stop serving and loving Him even if things didn't go my way. I am still going to be in love with you no matter what happens to my children, I love you Lord. You are my everything. I love my children and I love my husband, but you Lord is the best thing that ever happened to me and I choose you over any and everything in my life. If I lose everything, I still want you.

<u>I found comfort in the word of God</u>

By the time I finished telling God all about how I felt, I could just feel the spirit of God surround me to reassure me that no matter what the situation looked like, in the end of all of this, it is going to be all right. I whispered to God: Lord, I want to remind you of what you said in your word. You said, "many are the afflictions of the righteous, but you delivered out of them all (KJV). The word of God and a real relationship with God brought me through my dark season. Without the word of God and the power of God which comes through his word, I had nothing to stand on.

CHAPTER 5

The blessing of being connected to godly people

One of the things that kept me strong was the faith that I had been taught through the life and the teaching of my Pastor and his wife, Bishop James Swinson and Dr. Johnnie Swinson. They were examples of people who lived the scriptures in there day to day lives. They "walked by faith and not by sight". What a blessing it is to be connected to a church where the leaders walk and live by faith. I thank God for sending me to Waycross Georgia to a Church known as: Family Worship Center in 1988. God lead me to leave the church that I had grown up in as a child; Greater St. Paul Missionary Baptist Church and the leadership of Rev. Menefee and Rev. Johnnie Arnold. After I accepted the Lord and Savior Jesus Christ as my personal savior and I received the baptism of the Holy Ghost, I was on fire for the Lord. My Godly experiences came in the early years of my marriage. At first, it was difficult to do in a way because I was familiar with the people in my old church, but God had another plan for my life. He knew that I needed to be under the leadership that could identify with what I was going to have to go through. I am so glad that I obeyed God and connected to Family Worship Center/Faith Temple Ministries in Waycross, Georgia. I thank God that I heard and obeyed God's voice and moved despite what was comfortable for me. I will forever be grateful to the leadership of the Swinson family.

Bishop and Dr. Swenson's youngest son was diagnosed with Lymphoma at the age of 21. They too had stood and walked in faith and believed God in spite of the adversity that they faced. God had shown himself strong in their lives. God completely healed Rod Swinson of Lymphoma. He is now "Pastor Rod". He is a godly man, married to Marie Swinson and together they have 2 beautiful children. God has raised him up from Cancer and now he is an internationally known Pastor, teacher and anointed man of God. He is world renowned pastor and teacher, and author of the book *"Same Spot, Different Season"*. He now pastors Family Worship Center in Waycross Georgia. I am honored to sit under that great man of God and receive instructions from the word of God from him. I am blessed that he is now my pastor. His life has impacted mine and my family is so many positive ways. I love him and his family so much. This is a man that talks faith, but a man who lives faith. I thank God for giving me "Family Worship Center" of Waycross Georgia under the leadership of Bishop James Swinson and his Wife Dr. Johnnie Swinson and their son Prophet Rod Swinson, and his wife First Lady Marie Swinson. The Swenson's daughter, Pastor Tonya Swinson Hall has also been a powerful influence in my life. She is a true woman of God who is anointed for the end time. He ministry is reaching the far corners of the universe and I am so blessed to be connected to such a powerful woman of god. You can learn more about Pastor Rod and his testimony by going to his web site at thefwexperience.org. Pastor Tonya can be reached on all social media. She is now pastoring Victory Way Christian Center in Jacksonville Florida.

God connected me to some great men and women of God who taught me the word of God. I would like to encourage you to do something if you have not done so already and that is to ask God to lead you and help you to find a church and a pastor that God has specifically anointed for you and your family. You will need to be under good leadership and guidance especially if you are in a time of crisis and if your faith is being tried and tested. Without a doubt, strong spiritual leadership is essential to reaching your victory.

CHAPTER 6

Chelsea's Delima

When I had my daughter Chelsea, I just knew everything in my life was finally, perfect. I am finally here. It seemed like I had waited for her all my life. She was just what I had imagined. During the 5th month of my pregnancy, the Lord had given me a word of promise deep in my spirit. God spoke these words to me on night while I was praying over my unborn child: I heard him say, *"Daughter, the child that you carry is a child with great purpose and this child will speak the word of God from her mouth and nations will listen"*. I was utterly amazed. All I could do was worship Him. I knew that when I prayed and petitioned God for a daughter, I knew that he had selected a special one for me to mother, nurture, and train for God's Kingdom work. How honored and excited I was on the day that Chelsea Denise Young was born-July 11, 1997.

I now have the 3 things that I wanted the most. We were working and living our dream. Life couldn't be better. My son was 3 years old when Chelsea was born. Marvin and I had been married around 6 years. We were so in love as a couple and we were so proud to be the parents of these two beautiful children. At this point, we had our son and now a daughter; this was our dream come true. This was our happily ever-after. When my second child Chelsea was born, I thought she was the most perfect blessing I could have ever received from the Lord. She was born looking very healthy. She was beautiful and she was just what we had prayed and asked God for.

When Chelsea was 3 weeks old, the doctors told me that Chelsea was sick and needed attention immediately. Wow!! I could hardly believe it! Not my child. I am saved, I love the Lord, I do everything that I am told to do at church, no matter what. I couldn't be experiencing a problem; and certainly not one of this magnitude. Chelsea would not take her bottle, she did not cry, and she was lifeless. She showed no emotion at all. I would just look at her for hours. She just lay in my arms lifeless. What do I do? Should I panic? Did I do anything while I was pregnant that caused this beautiful baby to be sick? Should I just cry about this? Should I get mad at the doctors who delivered her. Should I be mad with God? My thoughts were in every direction. And somehow in this cloud of despair, I could hear the leading the Holy Spirit whisper; Wanda, remember the word of God says: "When my heart is overwhelmed, lead me to the rock that is higher than I" (KJV, Psalms 61:2). That's it, I thought. God is and will see me and Chelsea through this. I did not know at that time that there were more challenges to overcome. I just knew that I had to put all of my trust and confidence in the Lord God Almighty. As I began to take a stand in the Word of God and believe God for Chelsea's healing, one of the first scriptures that God showed me after I got news that Chelsea was sick was…"For this child (we) prayed; and the LORD hath given (us) our petition which we asked for him".

On July 31, 1997, I was at home enjoying my new baby after coming home from the hospital within 24 hours of her delivery. We had been home only two days, when we had a home visit from a home-health care nurse. Before I left the hospital, I had a few concerns about Chelsea, but nothing that I felt like we could not handle at home. Just to look at Chelsea, she was the picture of health. She was a beautiful. Oh, what a pretty baby. She had light pecan-brown color smooth skin. She had gorgeous carefully outlined pinkish looking lips that looked as if they had been brushed on. She had beautiful dark eyes and perfectly arched eyebrows that looked as if they had been drawn on by an artist. Oh, I was so excited!!!! My little girl. Oh,

I can't wait to dress her in pink and bows. Oh, her hair was beautiful. Dark, smooth, and a head full!!!!

My sister, Syble, and I discussed taking the Chelsea home; although the pre-natal nurse did not think it was such a good idea. She felt that we should wait until the baby could tolerate a full ounce of milk without falling asleep. I thought, well isn't that what babies do, sleep? I could not explain how inadequate I felt as a mom. My sister, Syble, who is also a nurse said, "She's fine, Wanda, she just needs to get home and get settled. I'll stay a few days and help you all get settled." That was all I needed to know. Let's go!!! I could hardly think about the hospital bills from having MJ and other times that Marvin, MJ and I had all been in and out of the hospital and emergency room. The nurse who was taking care of us suggested that we wait until the baby could at least hold 1 to 2 ounces of formula but we checked out anyway. At that point Chelsea was barely getting 1 ounce of food before she would fall asleep. I was torn between this nurse's advice and my sister's advice, but I decided to try it at home, so I was discharged to home within 24 hours of Chelsea's birth. I know now looking back what a bad decision that was, but like always, God was graceful and took care of us anyway.

It had been an interesting 3 weeks of having my new bundle of love at home. MJ was so excited. He would greet everyone at the door and in his 3-year-old voice, he would say, "come in and see what we got"! Oh my, life couldn't have been better. Everything was not perfect, but I was happy. I had my son, my daughter, my husband, and my good health. What else is there? Wow! How naive could I be at 38 years old? Later, I found out that there were many lessons, many afflictions and many, many tests of faith that I was to encounter in the days ahead.

A few of my friends stopped by to see me and the new baby. One Sunday afternoon, I noticed that Chelsea was really very fretful. She seemed to be trying to tell me something. She was hard to settle down, but nonetheless, I kept trying to sooth her as I saw fit. I thought that I was a good mama; after all, I had my grandma, auntie, my mother-in-law, and my husband's grandmother. And believe me all of these women were giving me advise, not to mention my neighbor, Mrs. Maudean who was like a mama to me.

Late, that Sunday afternoon, I was holding my beautiful baby girl in my arms and cooking at the same time when I happen to look down at Chelsea. I will forever remember the look that she gave me at 3 weeks old. She gently opened her eyes and looked directly into my face as if to say to me "don't ignore me, look at me and do something to help me get well or I won't make it much longer". When I think about it now, it is almost chilling that my child barely 3 weeks old was communicating with me and sending me an urgent message. As I look back, I realize that I was in so much denial. I think that somethings, we as believers think that things are always going to be perfect, but the truth of the matter is, God's will for us is perfect, but we will have to go through things at times of our life in order to get to where God wants us to be. God will process us to the right place.

I just couldn't or I didn't want to believe that anything was wrong with this beautiful baby girl. Finally, I realized about 9:00 p.m. that for the last 24 hours, for an entire day, my child had not eaten anything. This could not be good. Why is it that she had been either asleep or fretful for an entire day with no relief? Oh, my God! There is something wrong, what will I do? My mind started wondering, and I thought all sorts of things. What could possibly be wrong? What did I do?

The next morning, I got up early and I said to Marvin, I don't know where I am going, but I have to see a doctor. He said, "For what?" I said, "I don't know, Marvin, but this baby is sick and I have got to have someone look at her today." I called a dear Christian friend, Pam, who is a nurse and also worked for a local Pediatrician, Dr. Adrianne Butler, at that time. I said to her, "Pam can you see if Dr. Butler will see Chelsea today? I don't know what's wrong, but I've taken her to see her pediatrician several times and to be honest I think we have overlooked something. I don't know, but I believe that something might be wrong. The home health nurse suggested that we try to get another doctor to take a look. What do you think?" Pam said, "Let me check and I'll call you back." She called back about 20 minutes later and said, "Hey girl, Dr. Butler said can you bring Chelsea now?" I said yes, we'll be there." I did not even have any money on hand, but I gathered up my stuff and I got ready to go. The trip to Dr. Butler's office was a 5-minute trip. We left immediately.

Looking back over all the circumstances and events, Dr. Butler was sent by God especially for Chelsea. I believe with all of my heart that she was an assigned angel from God. Dr. Butler took one look at Chelsea and she took one look at me and she said, "You are exhausted, aren't you?" She said, "I want you to go home and pack a bag and get the baby and yourself ready I am going to make arrangements for you and Chelsea to get to Savannah's Memorial Medical Center I think for what we have going on, Savannah is better able to help you with this situation. Fighting back the tears, my voice trembled as I said, "Our situation, what situation, what's going on Dr. Butler?" She said, "I think something is going on with Chelsea's heart. Tears and thoughts of how, why, what, what if, filled my head. I said. "What?" She said, I can't be absolutely sure, but something is going on with her heart." My entire body went numb. I could barely think. I couldn't even move! I couldn't even think of a scripture, nor could I say one. OH MY!!!

Within a few hours, Dr. Butler had made all of the arrangements. The doctors in Savannah were just waiting for Chelsea to arrive. Chelsea and I were transported from the hospital in our hometown of Waycross, Georgia to the nearest children's medical center, which was in Savannah, Georgia. Savannah is about 120 miles from Waycross. It was August 1, 1997. A day I shall never forget. My beautiful baby girl was three weeks old. Exactly 21 days!! How perfect! Throughout the pregnancy, many wonderful and exciting things happened. It was a time that I felt especially close to the Lord. I prayed and talked to this child every day, even before she was born. Every Thursday at 4:30, I would go to the prenatal visits. At around 21 weeks of gestation, the doctor suggested that we start to listen and monitor the baby's heartbeat carefully, so he started to schedule my visits weekly instead of monthly. Every Thursday at 4:30 was scheduled. Since I had experienced some difficulty conceiving and delivering a baby in the past, I didn't think that this was such a strange thing to consider.

Why wouldn't we consider close monitoring of the baby? I really felt good about being watched so closely considering my history with pregnancy and delivery. Nevertheless, Chelsea Denise Young was born on July 11, 1997. It was very "normal" birth and delivery, or was it?

For a while, I did not want to even admit that there might be something going on with the baby, although, a part of me did recognize the signs of problems. Chelsea was diagnosed with a congenital heart defect that would require major surgery immediately. It was at this point that I had to admit to myself that my happily ever after was still a dream and not a reality. The truth was that the baby was very sick. Chelsea was born with a heart defect. Because of her heart defect, other organs in her body did not function properly. I had no idea that we would go through so much with this beautiful baby. I recalled a scripture that God had me meditate on during the pregnancy. "He desires truth from the inward parts" (KJV). The truth was, the baby was born sick and only my faith in God would get me through this trail.

Psalm 45:1 (King James) says; "My heart is indicting a good matter: I speak of the things which I have made touching the king: my tongue is the pen of a ready writer." I knew how to trust God, or so I thought. My life had not been easy up to this point by any means. I am the third child and youngest child. Both of my parents died while I was a child. My blind, 72-year-old paternal grandmother had become my guardian in 1970 when my father died of Kidney failure due to undiagnosed diabetes. My mother had preceded him in death. She died in 1965 of Paradises. My grandmother, whom we referred to as "Mama Roxie" and her sister "Etta Mae" raised me, my sister, and my brother. We were all 3 in our early teens when my dad died in 1970. These two elderly ladies took care of us until all three of us had graduated from college and were able to take care of ourselves. They were both remarkable women of God. My grandmother was an absolutely remarkable Christian woman and I dedicate this book in her memory (Roxie Cooper Carter, December 1, 1897- October 4, 1997).

The diagnosis was Congestive Heart Failure, a large ventricular septal defect and failure to thrive. All of the problems were secondary to what the doctor's called: CHARGE syndrome.

Say what? CHARGE syndrome? What is that? Can you fix it today and let us be on our way home? What does she feel? Is she in pain? Oh, so many questions!!!! What's happening to our baby girl? She was so little; she only weighed about 3 1/2 pounds; she was slightly peachy colored almost pale colored. Yes, still very beautiful, almost breathtaking and with innocence and peace. She lay there just quietly and helpless. My knees shook, my eyes filled with tears, and I reached way down in the inside and I pulled up a word: "by stripes, she is healed". NO weapon that is formed against her shall prosper, nay, in all these things we are more than a conqueror, the just shall live by faith and on and on and on I quoted the word of God as I remembered it.

I looked at my husband, Marvin; he didn't have an answer or solution. I listened to the reports of the doctors and they were overwhelming. I looked at my sister, who is a nurse and trained in the area of telemetry and all I knew was that something greater than anything in the hospital had to step in if Chelsea was going to live. What I started to meditate in the word and I remembered what Jesus said to the young girl who lay sleeping in Mark 4. Jesus gently told the girl to arise. He took her hand and said "talita cume". What he said to her was "damsel, arise". I spoke these words in her ears over and over.

I was desperate for some peace and some control; I began to meditate on the word of God. Oh, sure I was going about my normal day to day and to others I am sure that I appeared to be strong, but my strength was only in the Lord. My pastor had taught me that in the time of trouble, I was to "send Judah" first. "Judah" is another word for praise. It means to send praises up to God even in the mist of troubles. Now, you know that really doesn't make much sense if you ask me. My baby is dying and I am to focus my attention on speaking praises to God. Nevertheless, I did it! I would praise God all day long—quietly in my spirit. I cried out to God one night because my arms actually ached. I couldn't figure out why my arms hurt so much. Even though, I was 3-weeks post- partum, I was required to go on in God's strength. The Lord showed me that my arms ached because they longed to hold Chelsea in my arms. She was actually too sick for me to hold her and she appeared to be more comfortable swaddled in the hospital bed. I had to get a grip on things. I sat down and I remembered what the scripture said:

The tongue was the pen of the ready writer. I knew that if I could only write out a vision and run with that it would come to pass. I wanted a plan of action; I just wanted a plan.

CHAPTER 7

God Gave Hannah Samuel; He gave us MJ:

Chelsea had just gotten over her heart surgery. We were back home and we were so glad to be back on somewhat of a normal routine. I was thankful for everyday that I could go to work and leave Chelsea at the baby sitters. I knew that I should be thankful and happy that everything was going well for us finally. I began to thank the Lord for bringing us through all the trials and all the hard times that we went through and I wanted God to know I was glad the trials were over. As I was meditating on the word one day and just spending time in the presence of the Lord, I hear the words not yet. The Spirit spoke to me and said the trail is not over yet? Not yet? What are you preparing me for Lord? The Spirit of the Lord said, "This is not an ending but a beginning". I could not understand why I had to go through something else. But I know that God is a good God no matter what. This is what I call my YET moment of praise. When Jesus was getting ready to go to the cross, the bible says he cried out to God. He knew that the trial before him was going to be hard, but he also knew that it was something that I he had to go through. That is how I felt when I realized that I was still in the battle. I found comfort in the word of God in Luke and he withdrew about a stone's throw beyond them, where He knelt down and prayed, "Father if you are willing, take this cup from me. Yet not my will, but yours be done." Then an angel from heaven appeared to Him and strengthened Him. (Luke 22:42)

Around Easter of 1998, MJ started to be a little bit sick. It was nothing too severe, it was a fever, a cold, and a runny nose. I started to feel guilty because I felt that if I had been home and not in the hospital with Chelsea, I could have kept both of them well. I finally, at the advice of a dear friend, took M.J to a doctor. Thank God he was as thorough as he was. He did some test and the results were not what we expected.

We had just returned home from 3 weeks in the hospital with Chelsea after she had the open-heart surgery when M.J., our 3-year-old son, started to show symptoms of fever, runny nose, skin rashes, tiredness and other things that needed constant attention. It seemed like we were always on some type of antibiotic. He just couldn't get rid of the cold symptoms. We finally took him to see an ear nose and throat specialist. He did some test and decided that he wanted to take out his tonsils and adenoids. We agreed that perhaps that would help to alleviate some of the infections and therefore get rid of the flu-like symptoms. In all honesty, no matter what the ENT doctor said, I still had convinced myself that M.J. just had a really bad cold, or maybe it was a little pneumonia. I really felt that all he needed was to find a scripture to stand on, the prayer of faith, a round of antibiotics, some blessed oil along with some of mama's tender loving care and he'll be fine.

Nothing could have prepared us for the diagnosis that we got concerning our 3-year-old. The ENT did remove the adenoids and some other tissues from his nostrils. He told us that he wanted to just check out some things, so he needed our permission to have the tissues examined in a lab. His exact words to me and Marvin were, "I just want to make sure that everything was ok". So of course, we agreed to let him send the tissue off to the lab to do some tests.

Before the doctor left the waiting room, he turned around and crossed his fingers and looked directly into my eyes and said, "Let's hope for the best". He said, "call my office in a few days and I should have some results to share with you." Well, we did just that. About a week later, we found ourselves in the doctor's office waiting for the test results. It was at that moment that I felt a knot come up from my stomach to my throat. "OH!!! I am going to be sick", I thought to myself. What if M.J. is sick "for real"? I looked at Marvin, and he showed no emotion at all. The doctor entered the room with his nurse. "Mr. and Mrs. Young", he said, "thank you for coming in to see me today. I have some bad news." I thought to myself, what is happening to us, why is this happening to us, no not again, Please God don't make me do this again. I can't do this!!! No!!! I can't.... and before I could finish the thought, I heard that sweet voice again. "Wanda, whose report do you believe?" and immediately I said to myself, "I will believe the report of the Lord!!!" Again, the joy of the Lord came on me. Ok Lord, I don't know what you are doing, but I know that I will put everything in your hands and you said put you in remembrance of your word. So, nevertheless, at your word.

I had heard a word from my pastor at that time who was Bishop James Swinson, pastor of Family Worship Center. Bishop Swinson was known as a great man of faith. He was always inspiring and encouraging. Bishop was teaching in one of his sermons a message entitled "Nevertheless". I had taken hold of this message and has started to apply it to areas of my life. He talked about the fact that there are times when you will find yourself in difficult situation, but so did Jesus Christ. When Jesus was in the garden, it seemed like it was his darkest hour. But Jesus knelt down to pray. I started to be even more serious about my prayer time and my worship time with God. Bishop Swinson had taught me that praising God was a shortcut to my deliverance in any situation. I started declaring out loud each and every day that no matter what, God was going to get the praise out of every situation.

I started thinking and saying out loud, "Nevertheless, Nevertheless, Nevertheless, I am not going to give up and give in, but Nevertheless, Lord I trust you." Over the next few months, we faced some extremely difficult days, but when I look back, God was true to his word. He has never let me down. I will praise you and honor you for you have made everything beautiful in your own time. Nothing could have been more devastating—not even what we had just gone through with Chelsea having open heart surgery, now the doctor informed us that M.J. had cancer. The tissue from the adenoids went to the lab for examination. On Memorial Day weekend, in 1998, the doctor call and got Marvin and I out of church service to tell us to meet him Tuesday morning for an important meeting. Needless to say, by Tuesday night we were in the Pediatric oncology ward at the children's medical center in Augusta Georgia. Yes, you're right the tissue that was examined was cancerous.

Our precious little 3-year-old son had a rare form of Leukemia called Acute Lymphoblastic Leukemia often referred to as ALL.

ALL is a fast-growing cancer of the white blood cells. Lymphocytes are a type of white blood cell that the body uses to fight infections. In ALL, the bone marrow makes lots of unformed cells called blasts that normally would develop into lymphocytes. However, the blasts are abnormal. They do not develop and cannot fight infections. The number of abnormal cells (or leukemia cells) grows quickly. They crowd out the normal red blood cells, white blood cells and platelets the body needs. We thought that would solve the problem. At first, Marvin and I just literally fell apart! We did not know what to do. We cried, we prayed, and we were still faced with the dilemma. I remember calling my sister, Syble. When she answered the phone, the only word that I could utter was her name. I said, "Sib…" and I just broke down crying. Syble said, "Wanda, what is it?" I said, It's bad, It's MJ". She said, "Wanda, whatever it is, we are going to get through it together. God is going to see us through." Hearing those words form my sister meant more to me than anything anyone had said to me throughout the entire dilemma. I know that my big sister being a nurse would be there. I only had one need that was my need for prayer. Lord let my baby live.

The diagnosis of ALL was frightening. What a scary thought. Here is my oldest son, strong, happy and I thought was healthy and he is diagnosed with cancer. No, it can't be. But it was. We started chemotherapy the first round and everything was going well. After 24 hour of the medicines, MJ's kidney shut down and again, we were in P.I.C.U. Right across the hall from where Chelsea had her open heart a few months prior. Oh, what a day I thought. I thought I would go crazy.

CHAPTER 8

Talitha Cumin

Before I could begin to walk in faith I had to stand in Faith. When you really stop and think about it, it's a simple concept. You can't start walking until you stand up. I need to stand up or stand on something first. I needed something firm, and something sure. Naturally, I wanted to lean and stand on my sister, who was a nurse, and my big brother who had always been there to rescue me, and my grandmother, who I thought had the answer to everything, and of course my big strong husband who somehow could fix anything. But, none of these people could provide me with the foundation and the reassurance that I needed. The doctors didn't offer us much hope. I searched the scriptures for a word. What do we do, Lord? And what do we say? There were so many questions. The doctor's reports were frightening. Lord, Help me.

It was obvious that they were going to have to do surgery to correct the problems on both of the children. Two babies in the hospital at the same time. What will we do???? How will we cope?? Who? What? When? Oh, the mental anguish that I felt. It seemed like medical science did not have any answers for me. I felt myself slipping and falling apart. On the outside, I appeared to be ok. My friends and co-workers would remark, "girl, how do you do it?" Sometimes I would wonder myself, how do I do this? Just looking back on the situation, now I realize that it was just the hand of God and the spirit of God that surrounded me and kept me from going "off "and literally losing my mind. I am so grateful for God's mercy. It would have been very easy at this point to get angry with God, the doctors, my husband and everybody that got in my path, but I made a sound decision that I would not allow strife and bitterness to be a part of me. I will not tell you that it was not very tempting, but I choose to be at peace. I would quote the word of God that said: "He will keep you in perfect peace whose mind is stayed on Him…….

The one thing that I knew that I had to do was I had to give God praise. Yes, Praise. I had to tell God every day and all day in my mind and in my spirit what I thought about him. I remember that I reached a point while I was driving down the road on my way home from the hospital one day and I was just giving God praises and I said to God, "Lord, if you take the Children to heaven right now, I am not going to stop serving you and loving you, I am still going to be in love with you. No matter what happens to my children, I love you Lord. You are my everything. I love my children and I love my husband, but you Lord is the best thing that ever happened to me and I choose you over any and everything in my life. If I lose everything, I still want you". By the time I finished telling God all about how I felt, I could just feel the spirit of God surround me and reassure me that no matter what the situation looked like, in the end of all of this, it is going to be all right. I whispered to God: Lord, you said many are the afflictions of the righteous, but God delivered out of them all.

I will share this with every reader. The word of God and your real relationship with God will bring you through any difficult time that you are faced with. Without the word of God and the power of God which comes through his word, you will have nothing to stand on. Find the word of God and allow it to change you. The 'Joy of the Lord" will become your strength.

One of the things that kept me strong was the faith that I had been taught through the life and the teaching of my Pastor and his wife, Bishop James Swinson and Dr. Johnnie Swinson. They were examples of people who walk by faith and not by sight. What a blessing it is to be connected to a faith church.

I thank God for sending me to Family Worship Center. God lead me to leave the church that I had grown up in after my salvation. At first, it was difficult to do in a way because I was familiar with the people in my old church, but God had another plan for my life. He knew what was best for me and my family.

CHAPTER 9

Write the Vision

Several years ago, I woke up early one morning to hear what I believe was the voice of the Spirit of the Lord. It was a quiet, gentle, kind, voice. I heard these words, "Read Psalm 45:1. I didn't go and read my bible immediately, but somewhere throughout the course of my day, I read this passage of scripture. I took out my bible and I found Psalm 45. I read the first verse out loud. It said, *"My heart is indicting a good matter: I speak of the things which I have made touching the king: my tongue is the pen of a ready writer.* To be completely honest, I did not have a clue as to what this scripture was saying to me. I read the verse over and over again. I asked the Lord, "Lord, what does this mean?" I inquired and studied the scripture for the next several months and yet, I received no revelation from the Lord as to how this scripture was to be applied to my life.

It was not until I began writing this book that the Lord revealed to me what the true meaning of that scripture is for my life. The Lord used this word in Matthew to show me my call into the ministry. He showed me that I was to study to become a writer and that through my writings I would witness the love of Christ to the unsaved and the loss. I did not accept this call right away, but as I started to write this testimony of faith, I accepted the plan that God had for my life.

This is the ministry that God has given to me for this season in my life. I believe that I am called to be a witness to the ends of the earth by sharing my testimony through the writing of this work. For 3 years, I stood on the word of God in faith to believe God for healing from sickness and disease for two of my children who were totally healed by the Power of God. God has allowed me to share this testimony in this book. It was on the day that I hear the voice of the Lord, I believe that it was at that moment that the Lord was speaking to my heart and instructing me to write. This book was actually conceived on that day and is now coming about a few years later. I am writing this book to share my experiences as a mother to other mothers and fathers who may feel like giving up and giving in especially if the situations that you find yourself in seems to be overwhelming or more than you think you can bare. I have been there and you are not alone during this hour. I pray that you have found comfort through the reading of this work and that you will come to know that "If God be for you, who can be against you?"

This book is formed and framed using the word of God from: Matthew 28: 19 which says "**Go** ye therefore, and teach all nations…...." I accept this assignment and will walk in faith believing that God will use this book to bless and encourage someone and most of all, to encourage someone to give their life to Christ.

Now was the time in my life that I had to release my faith in God. I began to talk to myself and say: "Wanda, Get a Grip!!!!" My church family was so supportive. I could hear the words of my Bishop saying, "Sister, God has equipped you for this battle, remember what you have been taught".

I didn't have anywhere to turn. I began to speak over the situation and call those things that be not as though they were. I thought of the word of God in Habakkuk that said write the vision and makes it plain. I took out my pen and stood on the word that God had given me in Psalm 45: 1 that said: "…. The tongue is the pen of a ready writer….: It was at that moment that I answered to call of God on my life.

I wrote: M.J. I see you participating in school activities, going to college, getting married, working in your career, having children of your own, Chelsea, I see you at your 16th birthday party, falling in

Love, getting married going off to college, having your own family, and working in the ministry enjoying the Lord and enjoying Long life.

God has proven himself faithful to me over and over again. Yes, we went through some difficult times and I continue to face daily battles, but my faith in God, my committed life of prayer keeps me strong. Today everybody is well; today we declare in faith that this is the first day of the rest of our lives together. The best days for the Young Family are ahead. In 2001, God blessed Marvin and I again with a beautiful baby girl. We named her Jada Elizabeth Young. She is the absolute example of what God can do if you put your trust in him. She is free from sickness and disease and she is has brought joy to our family. Although, Marvin and I were well into middle age, when Jada was born, God promised that he would take care of us and that's what we believe.

CHELSEA TELLS HER STORY

Written by: Chelsea Denise Young

I have had many sad events in my young life, but what you have read was part of it, being forced out of the only school that I loved and due to go back but ended up not going and was angry over it, God is my strength and I have turned to Him in my time of tears.

I hope that my book will also inspire young preteens (ages 11 and 12) and all teenagers to stand up to mean people in the right way and learn how to defend themselves and that they will pray and stand tall in a school where the kids are often mean and disrespectful. I have a lot of advice for middle schoolers and high schoolers that I feel they should know and listen to because it will help them while they are in middle/high school.

Also, this book is dedicated to The Christian school that I loved so much, my love for you guys and your school made me want to write a book on how I loved you guys and how I wanted to come back and it is to thank you for being there for me, I love you all, God Bless You.

I want to help others that are in the situations that I was in 7 and 6 (respectively) years ago and I want to reach out to them because I am letting them know that they don't have to go through this, I want to see middle and high schoolers be ok and not have to be in a terrible school like I was for the 2011-2012 and 2012-2013 school years. I want to encourage them as well. This is my story of hope, forgiveness, and how I made peace with myself and how I now love family events even though they are long, this is my story that is about going from pain to joy, from hatred to love, from hurting teen to happy teen/young adult and you don't have to go through what I went through, YOU can be free from the pain and anger that This particular Georgia middle school caused me and my family, this story will help others. This is my story, this is why I wrote this book, I am stronger than this and I hope that you will be strong too. My diploma got here last year but I can help kids that are not there yet, SPED kids, I want you to be strong too. My story is a true story and I would also love to help SPED students too.

Dedication: This book is dedicated to: The Christian school that I loved so much, my friends Amber, Destini, Maleah (who I have known since the 1st grade), Mrs. Carr, to my cousin Taylor, my aunts and uncles, my other cousins, to all of the children that I know and other children, to the memory of my grandmother and my Aunt Syble, to my friend Abril and I give honor to my Lord Jesus.

I hope that this book meant something to you who are middle schoolers and that you will not be in that same spot but that you will be strong and that you'll trust God and that you will learn something from my story.

I love you all, don't let anyone tell you that you're ugly or a "female dog" because you are not that, middle school may be hard BUT it's worth it.

This is my story, I am Chelsea, the strong, the brave, the lovable!

I am strong, and you can be too.

Thank you for reading this book, God bless and keep fighting those middle schools and passing those tests and in high school, keep fighting and passing until you graduate.

God has given me the ability to write this for you and to tell you what you can do to avoid other events like what I went through and I want to help you remember:

1. You are brave
2. You are beautiful (girls)
3. God is with you

4. No one can tell you not to pray
5. You are stronger than what anyone says about you
6. You can graduate like I did

I know that middle school is hard, I know firsthand but I also know that middle school is not rainbows and unicorns.

I know what it's like to be called ugly or the B word, I know what it's like to be pushed and knocked in the arm, I know what it's like to be threatened by a teacher, I know what it is like to be put out of the classroom, I know what it is like to feel anger towards adults, I know what it is like to want to slap/hit adults including my own parents, I know what it is like to be lied on and controlled, I know what is like to be forced out of the only school that I loved and having my hopes of going back crushed, but I also know what it is like to forgive, to ignore mean words and to love. So, my advice for middle schoolers: don't forget your homework and your notebooks because I know that those teachers don't allow that because I have dealt with that, also tell your parents about your day at school.

To all parents, I highly recommend finding a good Christian School for your son or daughter and allow them to attend for their entire school years from PreK-12th grade. Hopefully, they go from prek-12th grade and you don't have to take your child out after a certain grade, you don't have to move your child, you can pay for them to stay there for the following (should Jesus tarry): 13 years (for kindergarteners) 7 years for 1st time middle schoolers, 6 years for 7th graders, 14 years, if you count preschool, 8 years, if your child is the 5th grade Middle schoolers: stay focused, set goals, have good attendance, explore career options, get involved in activities, study hard, ignore the strongly disliking, get good grades, and pray.

If your birthday is during the school year, ask that teacher to let you bring cupcakes or at least candy and have a birthday party or bring invitations for your party, middle school birthdays are usually 12th, 1st teenage year, 13th and 14th birthdays and we know that your 13th birthday is the 1st teenage birthday and it would be great for your class to celebrate it, in December, when it is close to Christmas, ask your teacher to give a Christmas party, just like you did in elementary school, have a Christmas party complete with music (the best ones are Jackson 5, Temptations, Hi-5, Dramatics, traditional and hymns), pizza, cupcakes, chips, gingerbread cookies, and gift exchange and no it is not babyish or childish, everyone can do this, and for 8th graders, ask your principal to give an 8th grade graduation if they haven't already and to give a party for the end of the year, This particular Georgia middle school never did this and I want local middle schools to start doing it and stop overworking the students, also on Fridays if you have finished all of your work and completed everything, ask the teacher that you're with to have a pizza party or to bring games to play and as for games, I recommend games that are clean and also don't listen to people who say that you're "too old". If their food is bad, bring your own lunch

Middle schools have Special Education as well so make sure that those SPED teachers do their job and also, it is ok to do online school for middle school too and homeschool lastly, show God to others.

For high schoolers: study, turn in assignments, keep up with classwork, check your locker when you need to, make all A's, if you love cheering, join the cheerleading squad, bring your lunch if their food isn't good, pray before class, go to Chapel services (Christian School), ask your principal to let your class have Thanksgiving lunch with parents/family members before the break and have a Christmas party before break in December and to have birthday parties if your or another student has a birthday during the school year, high schools have SPED too so if you are Special Education, meet with your SPED teacher when you need to.

Also, if you are in online high school like I did in 10th and 11th grade, make sure you take notes while studying and take breaks when you need to take one and if you sing, sing in school performances, also keep Christ 1st

High school is when students are close to their best friends and if you are, talk to them every day and study with them also.

This page is for elementary schoolers: you may be young, but you are in school, I loved elementary school and I loved the school that I love so much Christian as they have the best elementary/middle and high school curriculum but this is for only elementary schoolers. If you are in kindergarten (5 or 6 years old), this is your 1st year so don't be afraid, pray when you are nervous, do your kindergarten worksheets and help classmates, also take naps if you want during quiet time and enjoy the parties you have while in kindergarten

1st graders: this particular year is the grade where school gets serious so do your schoolwork, turn it in when you are finished, behave well, sign your name and the date on each worksheet, study for spelling tests, spell words correctly, make friends, and be kind to the other kids.

Multiplication starts in 2nd grade, and it is hard so study and get the answers right.

Elementary school is the best time to be at a Christian school so if you go to a school that teaches you about Jesus, take your Bible with you, go to Chapel services when they have it, pray before lunch, pray for others' prayer requests and say the Pledge to the Christian Flag (which I did at THE PRIVATE SCHOOL THAT I LOVED SO MUCH in 5th -1st time 7th grade).

Because you are in elementary school, I know that you have special parties for Christmas and end-of-year and do something special when a classmate has a birthday during the school year so I would say, have fun!

This page is for middle school girls: if ANYBODY calls you ugly, ignore it because you are beautiful as God made you beautiful, if any boy or even girl calls you that, IGNORE them, I didn't ignore it, because I felt so angry and nothing was ever done about it (This particular Georgia middle school), if ANYONE ever calls you the B word, tell someone, I told and all the boy who called me that during 4th block got was a referral, and the girl (during 2nd block) was told to apologize but the other kids didn't get any sort of discipline for calling me that word and I knew that it was false and when that coach told me to stop crying, I felt that he wanted me to be called that horrible word, but I knew better so if anyone says that word to you, you tell someone who may be a teacher, your parents, the principal, your TAA advisor or the school counselor, you are not the B word, you are beautiful.

Friends are important even in middle school, if you have a best friend that you are very close to and sit by at lunch or class, help them when they need help, pray for them, talk to them and follow the rules all at the same time, if you have a cell phone (and I am talking to middle school teenage girls), put it up during class and don't take it out until class is over, and stay close to Jesus and put Him first.

High school girls(all grades): if this is your 1st year in high school, don't be scared, you have been in school before it's just different this year, you're in high school and it can be tough but if you follow this advice you will be ok same for 10th-12th graders, 1st thing: do all of your schoolwork and turn it in on time, if you love cheering, join the Pep squad cheerleading team, and also, if you are graduating this year, make sure that you pass every test and have great attendance (try) and if you want to go to Prom (11th and 12th grade girls, you don't really have to go to prom to graduate), shop for dresses at your local mall, don't leave school to go get lunch, it's prohibited by the principal, our local schools aren't having that.

Ignore mean people, pray, read the Bible, go to Chapel services, apply for a Christian college or start thinking about attending one, have "Meet You at The Pole" day once a month to pray before class.

If you are SPED in high school, you may still need help so ask your SPED teacher for help at all times.

Trust God most of all and if you sing (good music), sing during their Christmas and Spring programs.

I am thankful that I graduated, Advice for middle school teachers: don't get mad when a student has to cough, let them excuse themselves and cough, don't overreact when a student has a situation with their stomach problem, let them step outside, if one of your students has to go to the restroom, let them go, don't get your students in trouble, discipline them only if they are doing something wrong and don't tell them not to talk about a school that they love, when I went through these things at that middle school, it was heart wrenching but I do pardon them.

Something funny happened one day while my mom and I were picking Jada up, someone yelled to Jada and told her that her "grandmother" was there to get her, I was not very happy about that because Jada is my sister, not niece, she is my mom's daughter (other), not granddaughter, mom found it hilarious but I felt that they should've said "your mom is outside" because she is her (and my) mom.

When mom told me not to tell my sister that she was no longer going to be at This particular Georgia middle school, I had to try hard to keep my mouth closed even though I wanted to tell her right away, we didn't care that it was going to be in 2nd semester and that she was about to become a teenager, we didn't care that she was close to some of the students, it wasn't about friends, or the grade that she was in, it wasn't about teachers or anything of that sort, it was not only passing that she needed to worry about, it was the fact that that middle school that I strongly disliked was too far anyways and that she needed to be in a school that was near her and so right before New Year's, her friends found out and she did too, she didn't like it but she had to accept it because we were done with that middle school that I didn't even want to attend.

She did well at the other middle school, she finished 7th grade and passed 8th grade and she is now a senior.

For seniors: congratulations on making it to senior year, my advice would be: study, get up early, eat breakfast, go to tutoring if you need to, go to youth group at church if you have one, go to bed on time, order your class ring if you want one, go to senior class meetings, ask for help in certain subjects, get a yearbook and walk across that stage

Also, if you don't want to attend prom, that is ok, I did but I only stayed 8 minutes and then went back home.

Senior year is also a great time to drive to school but be careful.

Behave because 12th grade is no excuse for bad behavior in class and that includes no talking out of turn, and put your cell phone up.

Senior year is a great time to have a Christmas party and a party before the last week because it is your last year in school.

That's all for high schoolers, God bless.

In middle school, I know that the day gets tough but hang in there because the day will be over before you know it, I speak about this because I care for you very much and love you, it is a great thing if you are attending a Christian school and they are teaching you the right way and Christian schools have Bible classes and Chapel services and if you are at this kind of school and you love sports, join the basketball team, the football team, the Cheerleading team and if you are interested in Band, join band class, you can also join Chorus in that Christian school

I want to give you encouragement, I encourage you to take your Bible to school and don't worry about what the teachers or other students have to say, also pray for your lunch before eating

In a Christian School, you certainly can't be stopped from praying and reading the Bible, and you can take your bible with you to lunch too, I say this because I am a Christian

Some events were terrible but I have to forgive and I also pardon those teachers/staff members and kids that hurt me at This particular Georgia middle school, I still know that This particular Georgia middle school is a bad school and I don't like it but forgiveness helps me feel better

I didn't let these events define me and I certainly won't let them define me now and I stand up for myself and I let God be in charge of my life as I'm not even in charge of myself, I let God take over my life. Teachers do indeed have a right to tell a student when to stop but only when it is necessary, I believe that teachers need to help students more, the teachers at the school that I love so much helped me and tutored me, I am all for after-school-tutoring in the mornings or afternoons and yes also both

What I want you to take from this is that for almost 2 years, I dealt with a terrible public school, dealt with hatred towards adults, anger, tears, pushing, teasing for the love I have for my favorite TV show, insults towards my favorite singers, being called ugly, and mean teachers but I forgave, loved again, graduated school and I am strong.

I am writing my story also because I wanted to get it out that school from 2011-2013 was a bad time for me regarding school but I am still here and I am glad to say that I passed school and wish all middle schoolers the best.

You can be ok, you don't have to be called ugly or any terrible cuss word name, you don't have to take being pushed at school, you can tell them to stop, don't be afraid to tell someone that you need help, I hope that the principal at your local public school puts a stop to name-calling and pushing so it would be a thing of the past because at This particular Georgia middle school, nothing was ever done for me, I pray that and the end of the school year that you do get an award.

My life:

I love eating, I love spending time with kids, I love listening to Michael Jackson and the Jackson 5 and watching Hi-5, Jon and Kate plus 8, Wilbur and listening to other Motown music, I also love to watch the tv show about monster trucks (Bigfoot Meteor/Mighty Monster Trucks).

I love Jesus and I love children.

My family and I spend a lot of time together, I am a daddy's girl and I graduated last year.

I wish I had graduated with the school that I love so much Christian School but at least I graduated and I needed to know what senior year felt like and I did back in 2016 I wanted positive things in my book too but I had to acknowledge what I went through in order to get to the positives of it and I had to expose the pain that This particular Georgia Middle School caused me and it was a part of my forgiving process and I am glad that I did and I said all of that to say this: school isn't easy at all and I know that there are people that are planning to quit school but I want to say don't give up, keep trying.

I do this not to defame anyone's character but to share the truth about this middle school and to expose it for what it is and to help others that have gone through having to attend a school that they didn't approve of, I am not a slanderer or a liar but I tell the truth and I pray that you forgive whoever did you this way in school if you ever dealt with that.

Another thing to middle schoolers: whether a teacher is nice or not, you have to obey but you can also move to another teacher and if you want next semester, move to a Christian school.

If you are attending a school that is not like This particular Georgia middle school, but is similar to a Christian school, I hope that you have fun, I am a high school graduate that is doing well and

I am glad to be sharing my story with all of you and I pray that you learn from it and not look at it as a "sob story" but see the happy ending in it and know that it is not a fairytale but it is my story to help middle schoolers that may have special needs, have been called names, have been treated unfairly by teachers and/or staff or want to move to a Christian school or online school and I want to tell them that it gets better.

Attending a Christian school: have fun, go to Chapel every week, pray, read the Bible, eat a good lunch, participate in Cheerleading or Basketball, love your teachers, and pass the classes.

I am a strong girl and I can handle anything.

In May 2013, I was officially done with middle school, and now I was about to start high school at the age of 16 (I turned 16 that July) and I was new to high school experience even though I was supposed to already be there, the 1st day of high school was that Monday, August 5, 2013 and although I wanted to be at the Christian school, I was happy to be done with middle school and was glad that I was now a high school freshman, I loved my teachers in 9th grade, they were very nice, one of them has a class for aspiring teachers (whether they plan to teach preschool or high school) and my mom was a teacher at the high school, in the cafeteria, they had varieties so if you didn't want a certain food, you could go to another, I still had trouble in Math so I received help in 9th grade math as well, in reading class, we had 2 teachers (both ladies) and they did a good job teaching and were also strict but kind, sometimes at lunch, I would go eat in my mom's classroom and other times, I would eat at the cafeteria, I did have to take quizzes and tests but studied hard for them, the other freshmen that were there had gone to school with me before and because I was 16 and most of them were 14 (others were 15), I was the oldest but didn't let that get in the way of learning and I made a new friend in reading class who was very sweet, only 1 time was I told to hush by the teacher and that December, the education pathway teacher was kind enough to let the class have a Christmas party also one day in History class, a girl asked who Michael Jackson was and I WAS NOT happy so I went on a 10 minute history lesson and she took it all in (how can you not know about MJ) also during

1st semester, the teacher (education pathway) took us (her class) to a few of the elementary schools here including the one right across from home and we also visited the preschool (the one I attended at age 5) and I read to the kids and we did fun activities with the kids and I loved that very much.

Then, in math class, before Christmas break, we had to take a math test and the math teacher was nice enough to play The Jackson 5's Christmas album and then we went on break and afterwards 2014 started and my sister became a teenager and started 2nd semester at the other middle school but to back up a bit, I started feeling ill and had to be home a few times but was still doing ok and this particular January, I was with a new science teacher and we ended up going to school 2 days that week and one of those days, the weather caused us to not have school and that same month, I went to the hospital due to not feeling well and also, because of my singing voice, I started going to chorus and that March, participated in their competition at school and then when April came, I started getting sick constantly and ended up on homebound, being ill wasn't fun at all during that time and I was asking for prayer all the time at that point and I would cry when I was sick and I would beg to stay home from school and when I was placed on homebound, I was happy because I finished the year early and I still didn't like going to school, I had had enough of school and was ready to quit school, also I felt that graduating HS 2 months before turning 20 was an oxymoron because everyone I know graduated either at 17 or 18 and turned 18 during 1st or 2nd semester (or during summer after graduating) and/or turned 19 after HS graduation August came (2014 of course) and my sister who had been a teen for only 7 months at the time, started her last year of middle school and my mother put me in online classes at online school for grades K-12th and so I was going to be doing school a different way, I no longer had to leave my home at 7:00 a.m. like I had been doing for 12 years (ages 4-16), I didn't have to be surrounded by noisy students and I could work at my own pace plus I could have my TV on during work and I could do it on the laptop and my brother was in college, my sister went to an actual school building (because she is close to her friends and she doesn't like being in the house all day) and my daddy was retired but mom still worked so it would be just us at the house and I loved it but I know that the teachers and students missed me and wondered where I was, (they always ask my mom and sister "where is Chelsea?") and whenever I was hungry for lunch, dad would get me something and sometimes I would cry when mom was gone (that should tell you that I have forgiven her) and I cry a lot but did my work, however when I would be done with my online school work, I would take a nap and other times, mom would make me come to the school and work on my assignments and so I would (dad would drop me off there) and the teachers that were online were teachers that I had never met let alone knew before and they were kind too and online school also meant I got to take breaks during the day (I love daytime) being out of regular school was a wonderful experience although I really wanted to go back to The Christian School that I loved and during breaks, I often and still do watch videos of Hi-5, Michael Jackson and listen to my other music as well, there were times that and I was finishing 10th grade and my sister was entering high school (9th grade) that March, the education pathway teacher let me come to her son's 1st birthday party so I did. Jada and I headed back to town and then my cousin who was going to be 18 that September, was leaving to go to college and so my siblings went with mom and Aunt Syble to get her settled and into her dorm room and that June I started online school in 2014, I had to participate and so I wanted to again for 2015 but we were at the family reunion and we stayed in the hotel 2 nights and then went home and I slept in the car because I had been up all night and then we arrived home and the next morning, Jada began her first day of high school and was excited and I was going to be in the 11th grade in online school again and was happy but at the same time wanted to be at the Christian School and 11th grade was good because I was at home online and at times, a lady would text me and ask me to get on so we could do reading together and we would and that same month and year just 4 years after me tests and the Math was hard too, but I tried my best and did well and mom still made me come to the school when I needed to, I was 18, in the 11th grade when I should have been in 12th or had I started Kindergarten at 5, college but I wasn't warming up to college now, I just wanted to graduate and be done with it, I really wanted to go back to The Christian School but ended up back at the high school for 12th but before I get to that, I want to tell the whole story, online school also meant that I could study online, but back up to that June, I went to my Goddaughter's 1st birthday party as well and fast forward to August of 2015, a 16-year-old boy in my mom's class (he was in the 10th grade) died during basketball practice and we were devastated, the whole community was and it was at the very middle school that I didn't like but I was heartbroken for them and we still miss this boy 3 years later.

Then in November, 2015, my parents, siblings and I went to Jacksonville, Florida for Thanksgiving lunch/dinner and we had my favorites: turkey, ham, greens and Mac and cheese and that same year. I still had a nice Christmas vacation then 2016 began and I was still in the 11th grade and in online classes ended up at the high school again for 12th grade that August and that was my only year of starting on a Thursday and it got off to a rough start, I had to go home that day but did ok the next day and the rest of that month and then September came and I prayed that the Board of Education would cancel school due to the weather before Labor Day and they did and this semester, my mom was one of my teachers and so I really had to do my work and I did but during September, I started having allergies and often ended up going home and that October, I was going to go to the homecoming dance with a boy in my Math class but he got grounded and I was hurt and decided to go home after the game (I went to game with my mom's friend and her nieces) I also, that same month, prayed again for no school before the break and God answered and then that November, my aunt wasn't doing well (the one that resided in Augusta and is Taylor's mom) and the 1st week, I went to the hearing doctor and stay home and then too, my Economics teacher had to be out of work because her mom was sick and the paraprofessional, who was a coach too took over the class and so did a friend of the teacher's niece and oftentimes, when I was done, I'd go back to mom's room and also one day during November, I took a vocabulary quiz and then the following Monday, I thought that the test was going to be the next day and got really upset about being told at the last minute and ended up in Mom's room for that class and not too long after that, she let me and some other students stay after school to do that test and then we had Thanksgiving break but the Friday that everyone got out, I went home early after eating pizza and also on Thursdays, my dad would come pick me up at 2:30 p.m. sometimes earlier and this was 2 years ago so it was a short time ago but back up to before November, the situation with my stomach had returned and I had to go home (but it was in mom's room) during November, my Economics teacher's mother passed and we were saddened by the loss but back up again, mom went to visit my auntie at the Augusta hospital the 2nnd Friday of that month and I stayed home but after Thanksgiving, the Economics teacher was back after so much sadness and she was stricter than ever but also nice and I let her be tough because she doesn't play at all and she was getting us ready for an upcoming test called the EOC and we had to study hard with no playing around especially if were graduating and getting up out of school and we studied and I often made the kids in my group desk laugh and one day, when MJ was mentioned, I got all happy and she knew and still knows of my love for MJ and then December came and that Thursday, we had to babysit the then 2 and a half-year-old son (I had also gone to his 2nd birthday party that March too) of my 9th grade education pathway teacher and it was crazy, I almost chose not to work with kids after that but I changed my mind 3 months later and another thing too, I was in the Fall concert with the Chorus class and loved that and Chorus was actually my favorite time of the day and I adored the Chorus teacher (she has 2 kids ages 8 going on 9 and 3) and we are friends on Facebook but back to December, that 1st Saturday, my parents both went to Augusta to see Aunt Syble who was still in the hospital and Jada was in the Christmas parade so mom's friend took me and her nieces to the parade and I heard several of my favorite Christmas songs on the floats including the Jackson 5 and my favorite rendition of Silent Night (Motown group that sang My Girl) and then Jada went home and I went with Ms. P and the girls (her nieces) and had some food and then mom and daddy came back and mom came to get me and I went home and was on my cell phone and I was heartbroken when I saw a Facebook post from Hi-5's Facebook page saying that the girls, one who had been in the group for 4 and half years and the other one who had joined after Lauren left 2 years prior and the one that joined back in 2013, were leaving but that same year, I was sad when 2 guys left the group and this time 3 girls and 1 guy were leaving and I was devastated and saddened by the news and screamed and told mom about it and cried, I was sad about it to the point where the next morning, I couldn't even get up to go to church (Sunday the 4th) and then the next day, I watched the Sunday morning church service of SBN's church and then my mother and sister Jada came to get me and took me to Ryan's for lunch and I believe it was to cheer me up after the heartbreaking news I had gotten the previous night and then we got home and decorated the Christmas tree and speaking of that, I wanted to try a white Christmas (you know that song) tree so we started using them the previous December(2015) and did again for 2016 and the next morning, Monday the 5th I told mom that I wasn't in the mood for any drama due to being upset and wasn't having it and we told the 1st teacher that was in the school and then class started and I told all of the kids including one who had driven me crazy all semester plus he was in reading class with me back in 9th grade, so I had known him for 3 years at this point and told the ones who drove me nuts to not even try it and I told them why I was so mad but I still had to do my schoolwork, mad or not mad and of course you have to do your work whether you're happy or mad and then that Thursday, we had the EOC, the day before that the teacher told us to get a good night's sleep and eat breakfast and so we had to do that and I took that test and passed it and also during this semester, I was moved to another room for math and did A+ and studied to get the answers right then the week after the EOC, I still went to school but it was close to Christmas break again and our community was praying for a young boy who was because he was ill and he was only 2 and a half so this touched me deeply and I had his prayer page on my Facebook, we were also praying for a teenage girl who attended the high school as she was also ill and then that week, I was in the Chorus Christmas concert and then that Friday, I stayed home from school and Jada went because she had to take an EOC test and the next day, Saturday, December 17, my Aunt Syble passed away that afternoon, when I went into my brother's (now old) bedroom to see daddy, I could tell something was wrong because he had his head hanging down in a sad way and told me the news. I am stronger than what any middle school or high school says about me, I am stronger than what I dealt with in that middle school, high school has its ups and downs but I didn't let it stop me and neither should you.

Now that I am home, I spend my days doing the same things I had been doing during school, listening non-stop to the beloved Michael Jackson and The Jackson 5, watching Hi-5 and my other favorite TV shows and living for God and spending time with kids and I love being young and being a young Christian is a wonderful thing and I have even considered taking my story to other schools because I know that there are other schools in the other states of the US and other parts of Georgia that are bad and they need help but there are also good ones.

So, with that being said, don't let high school get you down high schoolers, be brave, study hard and graduate!!

I hope that you take this advice and learn from my story and let it inspire you to do your best

God bless you and Don't let school get you down!

www.ingramcontent.com/pod-product-compliance
Ingram Content Group UK Ltd.
Pitfield, Milton Keynes, MK11 3LW, UK
UKHW022219230426
12048UKWH00016BA/945